Lunch Box Recipes

Fill Your Lunch Box with Delicious and Fun Lunches

By
BookSumo Press
All rights reserved

Published by
http://www.booksumo.com

ENJOY THE RECIPES?
KEEP ON COOKING WITH 6 MORE FREE COOKBOOKS!

Visit our website and simply enter your email address to join the club and receive your 6 cookbooks.

http://booksumo.com/magnet

https://www.instagram.com/booksumopress/

https://www.facebook.com/booksumo/

LEGAL NOTES

All Rights Reserved. No Part Of This Book May Be Reproduced Or Transmitted In Any Form Or By Any Means. Photocopying, Posting Online, And / Or Digital Copying Is Strictly Prohibited Unless Written Permission Is Granted By The Book's Publishing Company. Limited Use Of The Book's Text Is Permitted For Use In Reviews Written For The Public.

Table of Contents

Curried Turkey Wraps 9

Peanut Butter and Apple Sandwich 10

The Simplest Chicken Curry 11

Alternative Peanut Butter Sandwiches 12

Corn and Cashew Hummus 13

Banana Waffles for Lunch 14

Miso 15

Eggs Kimchi 16

Okonomiyaki 17

Tofu Mushroom Soup 18

Spicy Thai Pasta 19

Ramen Frittata 20

Caesar Parmesan Pasta Salad 21

Healthy Pasta Salad 22

Vegetable Pasta Salad 23

Grilled Pasta Salad 24

Italian Chicken Pasta Salad 25

The Best Italian Pasta Salad I 26

South American Pasta Salad 27

Pepperoni Rotini Pasta Salad 28

Linguine Romano Pasta Salad 29

Rotini Cucumber Pasta Salad 30

Greek Burgers 31

Chicken Burgers 32

Quinoa Burgers 33

Spicy Burgers 34

Spam Burgers 35

Chili Burgers 36

Salmon Burgers 37

Thai Burgers 38

Summer Soy Burgers 39

Provolone Caps Burgers 40

Crunchy Cheddar Bean Burgers 41

Thai Bell Bean Burgers 42

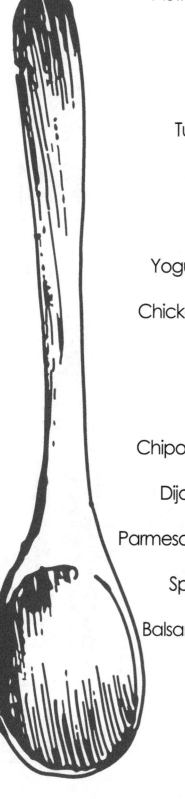

Authentic Texas-Mexican Enchiladas 43

Tex Mex Breakfast Brunch 44

Catalina's Salad 45

Tuesday's San Miguel Potatoes 46

Chipotle Burgers 47

Mexican Mac n Cheese 48

Yogurt, Parmesan, Basil, Turkey Panini 49

Chicken Breast, Zucchini, Pepper Panini 50

Turkey Provolone Ciabatta 51

Dessert Panini 52

Chipotle Pepper, Bacon, Spinach Panini 53

Dijon, Roast Beef, Roquefort Panini 54

Parmesan, Mozzarella, Chicken Cutlet Panini 55

Spinach, Turkey Ciabatta Panini 56

Balsamic, Parmesan, Mushroom Panini 57

Empanadas of Pineapple 58

Mushroom Empanada 59

Cheese Empanada 60

Picadillo Empanada 61

Empanadas In Argentina 62

Classical Empanadas II 63

Classical Empanadas III 64

Squash Empanada 65

Empanadas From Chile 66

Classical Empanada IV 67

Banana Empanada 68

Bacon and Onions Quesadillas 69

Restaurant Style Quesadilla Dipping Sauce 70

Mediterranean Style Quesadillas 71

Honey BBQ Chicken Quesadillas 72

Cinnamon and Apples Quesadillas 73

Chipotle Basil & Tomato Quesadillas 74

Steak and Onions Quesadillas 75

Authentic Mexican Quesadillas 76

Macaroni Salad 78

Classical Potato Salad 79

Easy Spinach Salad 80

Pecan Chicken Salad 81

Pear and Cheese Salad 82

Tuna Salad 83

Latin Corn Salad 84

Egg Salad 85

Curried Turkey Wraps

Prep Time: 5 mins
Total Time: 30 mins

Servings per Recipe: 6
Calories	452 kcal
Fat	32.2 g
Carbohydrates	12.6 g
Protein	27.1 g
Cholesterol	109 mg
Sodium	592 mg

Ingredients

- 1/4 C. white rice
- 2 lb. ground turkey
- 1 red onion, finely chopped
- 2 tbsp red curry paste, see appendix
- 2 tbsp tomato paste
- 1/4 C. water (optional)
- 2 limes, juiced
- 2 tbsp fish sauce
- 12 leaves lettuce

Directions

1. Heat a skillet on medium-high heat and toast the rice till browned lightly.
2. Transfer the rice into a food processor and pulse till powdered roughly.
3. Heat a skillet on medium-high heat and cook the turkey for about 8 minutes or until done.
4. Add the onions and cook for about 4 minutes.
5. Stir in the curry paste and cook till aromatic.
6. Stir in the tomato paste and reduce the heat to a simmer.
7. Add 1/4 C. of the water if the mixture becomes dry.
8. Stir in the ground rice and simmer for about 5 minutes.
9. Stir in the lime juice and fish sauce and remove from the heat.
10. Arrange the lettuce leaves onto a platter and top with the turkey mixture evenly.

PEANUT BUTTER and Apple Sandwich

Prep Time: 10 mins
Total Time: 10 mins

Servings per Recipe: 3
Calories	250 kcal
Fat	15.8 g
Carbohydrates	21.4g
Protein	8.5 g
Cholesterol	0 mg
Sodium	104 mg

Ingredients

1/4 C. peanut butter, or to taste
1 Gala apple, cored and sliced horizontally into discs, or banana discs

1/2 C. granola

Directions

1. Apply a coating of peanut butter to each piece of apple. Then top everything with some granola.
2. Lay two pieces of apples together, joining them at the granola and peanut butter.
3. Repeat with the remaining apple pieces to form apple sandwiches.
4. Enjoy.

The Simplest Chicken Curry

Prep Time: 15 mins
Total Time: 55 mins

Servings per Recipe: 4
Calories   339 kcal
Fat   22.9 g
Carbohydrates   9.3g
Protein   25.5 g
Cholesterol   74 mg
Sodium   95 mg

Ingredients

- 2 tbsp butter
- 2 tbsp vegetable oil
- 2 sweet onions, thinly sliced
- 4 skinless, boneless chicken breast halves, cut into cubes
- 2 tbsp curry powder, divided
- 1/4 C. coconut milk
- 1/4 C. chopped peanuts

Directions

1. In a large skillet, heat the oil and butter on medium heat and sauté the onions and 1 tbsp of the curry powder for about 5 minutes.
2. With a slotted spoon, transfer the onions into a bowl, leaving the juice in the skillet.
3. In the same skillet, add the chicken cubes and remaining 1 tbsp of the curry powder and cook for about 15 minutes, stirring occasionally.
4. Add the cooked onions and coconut milk and simmer for about 15 minutes.
5. Serve with a sprinkling of the chopped peanuts.

ALTERNATIVE Peanut Butter Sandwiches

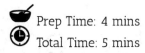

Prep Time: 4 mins
Total Time: 5 mins

Servings per Recipe: 1
Calories   373 kcal
Fat   18.1 g
Carbohydrates   43.5g
Protein   12.1 g
Cholesterol   0 mg
Sodium   502 mg

Ingredients

2 tbsps peanut butter
2 slices bread
2 1/2 tbsps marshmallow cream

Directions

1. Lay two pieces of bread flat on a working surface.
2. Coat one piece of bread with peanut butter, and another piece with marshmallow cream.
3. Now microwave the pieces of bread for 30 secs with the highest power setting.
4. Form the pieces into a sandwich and enjoy with milk.

Corn and Cashew Hummus

Prep Time: 5 mins
Total Time: 5 mins

Servings per Recipe: 3
Calories   270 kcal
Carbohydrates   28.6 g
Cholesterol   0 mg
Fat   16.5 g
Protein   7.8 g
Sodium   367 mg

Ingredients

two cups corn kernels, thawed if frozen
one cup cashews
one tsp. lemon juice, or more to taste
1/4 tsp. salt
1/4 tsp. onion powder
1/4 tsp. garlic powder

Directions

1. Place everything mentioned in a blender and blend it for about one minute.
2. Serve with rice.

BANANA
Waffles for Lunch

🥣 Prep Time: 10 mins
🕐 Total Time: 40 mins

Servings per Recipe: 4
Calories   241 kcal
Carbohydrates   47.3 g
Cholesterol   50 mg
Fat   2.5 g
Protein   8.3 g
Sodium   606 mg

Ingredients

one 1/4 cups all-purpose flour
three tsps. baking powder
half tsp. salt
one pinch ground nutmeg
one cup 2% milk

one egg
two ripe bananas, sliced

Directions

1. Combine nutmeg, baking powder, flour and salt and add milk and eggs.
2. Pour two tbsps. of batter over preheated waffle iron after spraying the iron with non-stick cooking spray.
3. Now place two slices of banana on the mixture pour another two tsps. of batter over these slices of banana.
4. Cook for about three minutes or until golden brown.
5. Serve.

Miso
(Bean Curd Soup)

Prep Time: 15 mins
Total Time: 35 mins

Servings per Recipe: 4
Calories   158 kcal
Carbohydrates   21.6 g
Cholesterol   0 mg
Fat   4.1 g
Protein   9.1 g
Sodium   641 mg

Ingredients

three half cups water
three tbsps. denjang (Korean bean curd paste)
one tbsp. garlic paste
half tbsp. dashi granules
half tbsp. gochujang (Korean hot pepper paste)
one zucchini, cubed
one potato, peeled and cubed
1/4 lb. fresh mushrooms, quartered
one onion, chopped
one (1two ounce) package soft tofu, sliced

Directions

1. Combine water, denjang, garlic paste, dashi and gochujang in saucepan over medium heat and let it boil for two minutes.
2. Now add zucchini, potato, onions and mushrooms, and cook for another 7 minutes.
3. Now add tofu and cook until tender.

EGGS
Kimchi

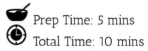

Prep Time: 5 mins
Total Time: 10 mins

Servings per Recipe: 4
Calories   208 kcal
Carbohydrates   3.5 g
Cholesterol   186 mg
Fat   18.8 g
Protein   7.5 g
Sodium   568 mg

Ingredients

two tbsps. vegetable oil
one cup kimchi, or to taste
two large eggs, beaten

Directions

1. Cook kimchi in hot oil over medium heat for about two minutes and add eggs, and cook for another three minutes to get the eggs tender.
2. Serve.

Okonomiyaki (Variety Pancake) (お好み焼き)

Prep Time: 15 mins
Total Time: 45 mins

Servings per Recipe: 4
Calories   659 kcal
Carbohydrates   90.7 g
Cholesterol   217 mg
Fat   19.4 g
Protein   29.3 g
Sodium   1531 mg

Ingredients

- 12 ounces sliced bacon
- 1 1/3 cups water
- 4 eggs
- 3 cups all-purpose flour
- 1 tsp salt
- 1 medium head cabbage, cored and sliced
- 2 tbsps minced pickled ginger
- 1/4 cup tonkatsu sauce or barbeque sauce

Directions

1. Get a frying pan. Bacon should be fried with a medium heat. Soak excess oils with paper towel and put to the side.
2. Get a bowl. Combine some water and eggs. Next combine in slowly, your flour, and then add salt.
3. Combine with the flour: the ginger, and cabbage and mix until even.
4. Get a 2nd frying pan or use the one from earlier. Add some nonstick spray to it. Take 1/4 cup of batter and put it in the middle of the pan.
5. Cover the batter with 4 bacon strips. Make sure the batter is circular. Fry for 6 mins. Turn over the batter and cook the opposite side until golden. Set aside.
6. Garnish with tonkatsu sauce. Cook all the batter in the same manner.
7. Enjoy.

TOFU Mushroom Soup (豆腐のキノコのスープ)

 Prep Time: 10 mins
Total Time: 20 mins

Servings per Recipe: 2
Calories   100 kcal
Carbohydrates   4.8 g
Cholesterol   3 mg
Fat   3.9 g
Protein   11 g
Sodium   1326 mg

Ingredients

3 cups prepared dashi stock
1/4 cup sliced shiitake mushrooms
1 tbsp miso paste
1 tbsp soy sauce
1/8 cup cubed soft tofu

1 green onion, diced

Directions

1. Get a saucepan. Add your stock, get it boiling. Once boiling add mushrooms and cook for 4 mins.
2. Get a bowl. Combine soy sauce and miso paste evenly. Mix this with your stock.
3. For 6 mins let broth cook. Add some diced green onion.
4. Enjoy.

Spicy Thai Pasta

Prep Time: 15 mins
Total Time: 20 mins

Servings per Recipe: 8
Calories	564 kcal
Carbohydrates	52.4 g
Cholesterol	230 mg
Fat	19.3 g
Protein	46.3 g
Sodium	375 mg

Ingredients

1 (12 ounce) package rice vermicelli
1 large tomato, diced
2 pounds cooked shrimp, peeled and deveined
4 green onions, diced
1 1/2 cups prepared Thai peanut sauce

Directions

1. Add rice vermicelli into boiling water and cook for about five minutes or until done.
2. Combine this rice with tomato, peanut sauce, green onions and shrimp very thoroughly in a medium sized bowl before refrigerating for at least eight hours.

RAMEN
Frittata

Prep Time: 5 mins
Total Time: 20 mins

Servings per Recipe: 4
Calories   339 kcal
Carbohydrates   28.8 g
Cholesterol   302 mg
Fat   15.7 g
Protein   20.3 g
Sodium   681 mg

Ingredients

2 (3 ounce) packages chicken flavored ramen noodles
6 eggs
2 tsps butter
1/2 cup shredded Cheddar cheese

Directions

1. Cook ramen noodles in boiling water for about 2 minutes and drain it with the help of colander.
2. Pour the mixture of eggs and content of seasoning packets over noodles before cooking this in hot butter for about seven minutes.
3. Turn it over after cutting it into four slices and brown both sides.
4. Put some cheese over the top before serving.

Caesar Parmesan Pasta Salad

Prep Time: 15 mins
Total Time: 30 mins

Servings per Recipe: 12
Calories   291 kcal
Carbohydrates   32.6 g
Cholesterol   6 mg
Fat   14.6 g
Protein   8.5 g
Sodium   728 mg

Ingredients

1 (16 ounce) package rotini pasta
1 cup Italian-style salad dressing
1 cup creamy Caesar salad dressing
1 cup grated Parmesan cheese
1 red bell pepper, diced
1 green bell pepper, chopped
1 red onion, diced

Directions

1. Cook pasta in salty boiling water for about 10 minutes until tender before draining it.
2. Mix pasta, red bell pepper, Italian salad dressing, Caesar dressing, Parmesan cheese, green bell pepper and red onion very thoroughly before refrigerating for a few hours.
3. Serve.

HEALTHY
Pasta Salad

Prep Time: 15 mins
Total Time: 30 mins

Servings per Recipe: 12
Calories	289 kcal
Carbohydrates	34.6 g
Cholesterol	8 mg
Fat	13.9 g
Protein	10 g
Sodium	764 mg

Ingredients

1 (16 ounce) package uncooked rotini pasta
1 (16 ounce) bottle Italian salad dressing
2 cucumbers, chopped
6 tomatoes, chopped
1 bunch green onions, chopped
4 ounces grated Parmesan cheese
1 tbsp Italian seasoning

Directions

1. Cook pasta in salty boiling water for about 10 minutes until tender before draining it.
2. Coat a mixture of pasta, green onions, cucumbers and tomatoes with a mixture of parmesan cheese and Italian seasoning very thoroughly before refrigerating it covered for a few hours.
3. Serve.

Vegetable Pasta Salad

Prep Time: 10 mins
Total Time: 25 mins

Servings per Recipe: 8
Calories	181 kcal
Carbohydrates	38.1 g
Cholesterol	0 mg
Fat	0.7 g
Protein	5.4 g
Sodium	238 mg

Ingredients

- 10 ounces fusilli pasta
- 1 onion, chopped
- 1 green bell pepper, chopped
- 2 tomatoes, chopped
- 1 cup chopped mushrooms
- 3/4 cup fat free Italian-style dressing

Directions

1. Cook pasta in salty boiling water for about 10 minutes until tender before draining it.
2. Mix pasta, mushrooms, onions, tomatoes and bell pepper very thoroughly before refrigerating for at least one hour.
3. Serve.

GRILLED Pasta Salad

Prep Time: 15 mins
Total Time: 45 mins

Servings per Recipe: 4
Calories   504 kcal
Carbohydrates   48 g
Cholesterol   103 mg
Fat   13.2 g
Protein   46.5 g
Sodium   650 mg

Ingredients

4 skinless, boneless chicken breast halves
steak seasoning to taste
8 ounces rotini pasta
8 ounces mozzarella cheese, cubed
1 red onion, chopped
1 head romaine lettuce, chopped
6 cherry tomatoes, chopped

Directions

1. At first you need to set grill at medium heat and put some oil before starting anything else.
2. Coat chicken breast with steak seasoning before cooking it on the preheated grill for 8 minutes each side.
3. Cook pasta in salty boiling water for about 10 minutes until tender before draining it.
4. Add mixture of tomatoes, cheese, onion and lettuce into the bowl containing pasta and chicken.
5. Mix it thoroughly before serving.

Italian Chicken Pasta Salad

Prep Time: 10 mins
Total Time: 2 hrs 25 mins

Servings per Recipe: 6
Calories   218 kcal
Carbohydrates   20.4 g
Cholesterol   18 mg
Fat   11.4 g
Protein   9.6 g
Sodium   654 mg

Ingredients

- 1 cup seashell pasta
- 1 cup chopped, cooked chicken meat
- 3 green onions, chopped into 1 inch pieces
- 1 red bell pepper, chopped
- 1 cup sliced black olives
- 1 cucumber, peeled and chopped
- 2/3 cup Italian-style salad dressing
- 1/4 cup sunflower seeds(optional)

Directions

1. Cook pasta in salty boiling water for about 10 minutes until tender before draining it.
2. Coat mixture of pasta, bell pepper, chicken, green onions, olives and cucumber with dressing very thoroughly before refrigerating for at least 2 hours.
3. Serve.

THE BEST
Italian Pasta Salad I

Prep Time: 15 mins
Total Time: 25 mins

Servings per Recipe: 12
Calories	371 kcal
Carbohydrates	29.2 g
Cholesterol	46 mg
Fat	21 g
Protein	15.2 g
Sodium	1893 mg

Ingredients

1 (12 ounce) package tri-color rotini pasta
3/4 pound Italian salami, finely diced
1/2 green bell pepper, sliced
1/2 red bell pepper, sliced
1/2 red onion, chopped
1 cup Italian-style salad dressing
1 (6 ounce) can sliced black olives
8 ounces small fresh mozzarella balls (ciliegine)
3 (.7 ounce) packages dry Italian-style salad dressing mix, or to taste
1/2 cup shredded Parmesan cheese

Directions

1. Cook pasta in salty boiling water for about 10 minutes until tender before draining it.
2. Coat mixture of pasta, red bell pepper, salami, green bell pepper, onion, salad dressing, olives, and mozzarella cheese with dry salad dressing very thoroughly before refrigerating for at least 2 hours.
3. Sprinkle some parmesan cheese before serving.

South American Pasta Salad

Prep Time: 10 mins
Total Time: 40 mins

Servings per Recipe: 6
Calories	618 kcal
Carbohydrates	46.4 g
Cholesterol	68 mg
Fat	38.4 g
Protein	22.8 g
Sodium	980 mg

Ingredients

- 2 cups spiral pasta
- 1 pound ground beef
- 1 (1.25 ounce) package taco seasoning
- 3 cups shredded lettuce
- 2 cups halved cherry tomatoes
- 1 cup shredded Cheddar cheese
- 1/2 cup chopped onion
- 1/2 cup French salad dressing
- 1 (7 ounce) bag corn chips
- 2 tbsps sour cream

Directions

1. Cook pasta in salty boiling water for about 10 minutes until tender before draining it.
2. Cook ground beef in a large skillet for about 10 minutes or until you see that it is no longer pink from the center before stirring in taco seasoning.
3. Coat mixture of pasta and beef with mixture lettuce, French dressing, tomatoes, Cheddar cheese, onion and corn chips very thoroughly before refrigerating for at least 2 hours.
4. Add some sour cream at the top before serving.

PEPPERONI
Rotini Pasta Salad

Prep Time: 15 mins
Total Time: 2 hrs 25 mins

Servings per Recipe: 8
Calories   415 kcal
Carbohydrates   25.6 g
Cholesterol   33 mg
Fat   29.1 g
Protein   13.9 g
Sodium   1518 mg

Ingredients

1 (16 ounce) package tri-color rotini pasta
1/4 pound sliced pepperoni sausage
1 cup fresh broccoli florets
1 (6 ounce) can black olives, drained and sliced
1 (8 ounce) package mozzarella cheese, shredded
1 (16 ounce) bottle Italian-style salad dressing

Directions

1. Cook pasta in salty boiling water for about 10 minutes until tender before draining it.
2. Mix pasta, dressing, pepperoni, cheese, broccoli and olives very thoroughly before refrigerating for at least an hour.
3. Serve.

Linguine Romano Pasta Salad

Prep Time: 15 mins
Total Time: 35 mins

Servings per Recipe: 6
Calories   275 kcal
Carbohydrates   32.2 g
Cholesterol   10 mg
Fat   12.8 g
Protein   9.9 g
Sodium   141 mg

Ingredients

1 (8 ounce) package linguine pasta
1 (12 ounce) bag broccoli florets, cut into bite-size pieces
1/4 cup olive oil
4 tsps minced garlic
1/2 tsp red pepper flakes
1/2 cup finely shredded Romano cheese
2 tbsps finely chopped fresh flat-leaf parsley
1/4 tsp ground black pepper
salt to taste

Directions

1. Cook linguine in salty boiling water for about 10 minutes until tender before draining it.
2. Steam broccoli for about 5 minutes with the help of steamer insert in a saucepan.
3. Cook garlic and red pepper flakes in hot oil for about 3 minutes before adding this and broccoli to the pot containing linguine.
4. Stir in Romano cheese, salt, parsley and black pepper.
5. Combine thoroughly before serving.

ROTINI Cucumber Pasta Salad

 Prep Time: 15 mins
Total Time: 2 hrs 30 mins

Servings per Recipe: 8
Calories 297 kcal
Carbohydrates 43.9 g
Cholesterol 0 mg
Fat 10.6 g
Protein 7.2 g
Sodium 608 mg

Ingredients

- 14 ounces uncooked rotini pasta
- 2 cucumbers, chopped
- 1/2 onion, finely chopped
- 10 cherry tomatoes, quartered
- 3/4 cup pitted black olives, sliced
- 1 cup Italian-style salad dressing

Directions

1. Cook rotini in salty boiling water for about 10 minutes until tender before draining it.
2. Coat a mixture of pasta, olives, cucumbers, tomatoes and onion with Italian dressing very thoroughly before refrigerating for at least two hours.
3. Serve.

Greek Burgers

Prep Time: 25 mins
Total Time: 1 hr 35 mins

Servings per Recipe: 8
Calories	479 kcal
Carbohydrates	26.2 g
Cholesterol	81 mg
Fat	30.4 g
Protein	23.9 g
Sodium	559 mg

Ingredients

- 1/2 cup mayonnaise
- 1 tsp minced garlic
- 2 lbs ground lamb
- 1/4 cup breadcrumbs
- 1 cup trimmed, diced fennel bulb
- 3 tbsps shallots, minced
- 1 tsp dried oregano
- 1/2 tsp salt
- ground black pepper to taste
- 1 tbsp olive oil
- 8 hamburger buns

Directions

1. Mix mayonnaise with some minced garlic and then cover it before putting it into the refrigerator for an hour
2. Set a grill or grill plate at medium heat and put some oil before continuing.
3. Take out lamb, fennel, shallots, breadcrumbs, oregano, and salt, and then mix it thoroughly.
4. Form some patties that are ¾ inch and then sprinkle some black pepper over it.
5. Now place burgers on the grill or grilling plate and cook them for about 4 minutes on each side. If using a grill plate increase the cooking time until burgers are medium or medium well.
6. Serve the previously prepared mixture on buns.

CHICKEN
Burgers

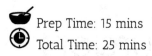

Prep Time: 15 mins
Total Time: 25 mins

Servings per Recipe: 6
Calories   368 kcal
Carbohydrates   67.8 g
Cholesterol   27 mg
Fat   8.1 g
Protein   11 g
Sodium   705 mg

Ingredients

1 egg
1 onion, finely chopped
1 lb ground chicken
1 tsp ground cumin
1 tsp celery seed
1 tsp salt
1/2 cup quick-cooking oats
4 slices whole-grain bread, torn into chunks
2 tbsps canola oil

Directions

1. Put some bread in a blender and blend until you have some really nice bread crumbs.
2. Mix cumin, salt, celery seed, oats, mustard and bread crumbs together in a small bowl and also egg, chicken, and onion in a separate bowl.
3. Mix both these mixtures together and then shape this mixture into 6 patties.
4. Now put some oil in a large skillet and cook patties until they are brown on each side and tender

Quinoa Burgers

Prep Time: 15 mins
Total Time: 35 mins

Servings per Recipe: 9
Calories   169 kcal
Carbohydrates   22.4 g
Cholesterol   86 mg
Fat   5.2 g
Protein   8.1 g
Sodium   270 mg

Ingredients

2 1/2 cups cooked quinoa (at room temperature)
4 eggs, beaten
1 sweet yellow onion, finely chopped
1/3 cup freshly grated Parmesan cheese
3 cloves garlic, finely chopped
1/2 tsp fine sea salt
1 cup whole-grain bread crumbs
1 tsp butter, or as needed

Directions

1. Take out quinoa, yellow onion, Parmesan cheese, eggs, garlic, and sea salt in an appropriate bowl and then mix together.
2. Also add some bread crumbs and mix again.
3. Make 9 patties and cook in melted butter until crispy on both sides.

SPICY Burgers

🥣 Prep Time: 15 mins
🕐 Total Time: 25 mins

Servings per Recipe: 6
Calories   232 kcal
Carbohydrates   1.1 g
Cholesterol   70 mg
Fat   16.4 g
Protein   19.1 g
Sodium   67 mg

Ingredients

1 tsp ground cumin
2 tbsps chopped fresh cilantro
1 tsp crushed red pepper flakes
1 fresh habanero pepper, seeded and minced (optional)
1 small fresh poblano chile pepper, seeded and minced
2 fresh jalapeno peppers, seeded and minced
2 tsps minced garlic
2 lbs ground beef

Directions

1. Set grill or grilling plate at medium heat and put some oil before continuing.
2. Take out a large bowl and mix beef, jalapeno peppers, poblano pepper, garlic, red pepper flakes, cilantro, habanero pepper and cumin.
3. Make burger patties from this mixture and cook them on the heated grill for about 5 minutes each side.
4. NOTE: If using a grilling plate then increase the cooking time of the meat until your appropriate tenderness has been achieved.

Spam Burgers

Prep Time: 10 mins
Total Time: 20 mins

Servings per Recipe: 4
Calories   268 kcal
Carbohydrates   12.9 g
Cholesterol   92 mg
Fat   10.9 g
Protein   27.8 g
Sodium   484 mg

Ingredients

- 1 (12 ounce) container fully cooked luncheon meat (e.g. Spam)
- 4 hard-cooked eggs
- 4 ounces Cheddar cheese, cubed
- 1 medium onion, chopped
- 3 tbsps mayonnaise
- 6 slices bacon, cut in half
- 6 hamburger buns, split

Directions

1. Heat up your broiler before continuing.
2. Now add cheese, onion and spam in the blender, and blend.
3. After blending mix some mayonnaise in.
4. Now spread the mixture equally in the buns and also add two bacon pieces on top of each layer of meat.
5. Now put buns and meat spread into the preheated oven for about 7 minutes and serve.

CHILI Burgers

Prep Time: 5 mins
Total Time: 20 mins

Servings per Recipe: 8
Calories	230 kcal
Carbohydrates	3.7 g
Cholesterol	63 mg
Fat	15.4 g
Protein	18.3 g
Sodium	486 mg

Ingredients

- salt and pepper to taste
- 1/3 cup tomato-based chili sauce
- 1/2 lb Italian sausage
- 1 1/2 lbs ground beef

Directions

1. First, set a grill or grilling plate at medium heat and put some oil before continuing.
2. Get a bowl of medium sized and mix Italian sausage, salt, pepper, beef and some chili sauce together.
3. Now make 8 patties out of this and grill these patties for about 8 minutes on each side before serving.
4. NOTE: If using a grilling plate then increase the cooking time of the meat until your appropriate tenderness has been achieved.

Salmon Burgers

Prep Time: 10 mins
Total Time: 25 mins

Servings per Recipe: 4
Calories   268 kcal
Carbohydrates   12.9 g
Cholesterol   92 mg
Fat   10.9 g
Protein   27.8 g
Sodium   484 mg

Ingredients

1 (14.75 ounce) can salmon, drained and flaked
3/4 cup rolled oats
1/2 onion, sliced
1/2 lemon, juiced
1 egg
1 tbsp Dijon mustard
salt and ground black pepper to taste
1 tsp vegetable oil

Directions

1. Take out salmon, onion, egg, lemon juice, mustard, oats salt, and black pepper, and mix it thoroughly.
2. Now make 4 patties out of this mixture and cook in hot oil for about 7 minutes on each side before serving.

THAI Burgers

🥣 Prep Time: 30 mins
⏱ Total Time: 36 mins

Servings per Recipe: 6
Calories   438 kcal
Carbohydrates   12.5 g
Cholesterol   99 mg
Fat   31 g
Protein   26.6 g
Sodium   160 mg

Ingredients

1 3/4 lbs lean ground beef
1/2 cup bread crumbs
2 tbsps lemon grass, minced
2 tbsps chopped fresh basil
2 tbsps minced shallots
2 red chili peppers, seeded and minced
1/4 cup chopped peanuts
salt and pepper to taste
2 limes

Directions

1. At first set a grill or grilling plate to a medium heat and put some oil before continuing.
2. Remove bread crumbs, shallot, lemon grass, chili pepper, ground round and peanuts, and mix them efficiently before adding salt and pepper into it.
3. Now make some patties out of this mixture and place these patties on the preheated grill for about 4 minutes each side.
4. NOTE: If using a grilling plate then increase the cooking time of the meat until your appropriate tenderness has been achieved.

Summer Soy Burgers

🥣 Prep Time: 15 mins
⏲ Total Time: 20 mins

Servings per Recipe: 8
Calories   193 kcal
Fat   4.3 g
Carbohydrates   31.9 g
Protein   6.9 g

Ingredients

- 2 tsp olive oil
- 1 small onion, grated
- 2 cloves crushed garlic
- 2 carrots, shredded
- 1 small summer squash, shredded
- 1 small zucchini, shredded
- 1 1/2 C. rolled oats
- 1/4 C. shredded Cheddar cheese
- 1 egg, beaten
- 1 tbsp soy sauce
- 1 1/2 C. all-purpose flour

Directions

1. Before you do anything heat the grill and grease it.
2. Place a large skillet on medium heat. Add the oil and heat it. Stir in the onion with garlic and cook them for 6 min.
3. Add the carrots, squash, and zucchini then cook them for 3 min. turn off the heat. Stir in the oats, cheese, soy sauce, egg, salt and pepper.
4. Get a mixing bowl: Add the veggies mix to the bowl and cover it. Place it in the fridge for 1 h 15 min. Shape the mix into 8 cakes.
5. Spoon the flour into a dish. Dust the veggies burgers with flour and cook them in the grill for 6 min on each side.
6. Serve your burgers with your favorite toppings.

PROVOLONE
Caps Burgers

Prep Time: 15 mins
Total Time: 35 mins

Servings per Recipe: 4
Calories 203 kcal
Fat 14.6 g
Carbohydrates 9.8g
Protein 10.3 g
Cholesterol 20 mg
Sodium 259 mg

Ingredients

4 Portobello mushroom caps
1/4 C. balsamic vinegar
2 tbsps olive oil
1 tsp dried basil
1 tsp dried oregano
1 tbsp minced garlic

Salt and pepper to taste
4 (1 ounce) slices provolone cheese

Directions

1. Before you do anything heat the grill and grease it.
2. Get a mixing bowl: Add the vinegar, oil, basil, oregano, garlic, salt, and pepper. Mix them well to make the marinade.
3. Stir the mushroom into the marinade. Place it aside for 18 min. Drain the mushroom and place the marinade aside.
4. Cook the mushroom caps on the grill for 7 min on each side while basting them with the marinade every 2 min. Place the cheese slices on the mushroom while it is hot to melt.
5. Assemble your burgers with your favorite toppings.
6. Enjoy.

Crunchy Cheddar Bean Burgers

Prep Time: 15 mins
Total Time: 25 mins

Servings per Recipe: 4
Calories   297 kcal
Fat   20.1 g
Carbohydrates   18.5g
Protein   10.7 g
Cholesterol   61 mg
Sodium   526 mg

Ingredients

- 1 (15 ounce) can butter beans, drained
- 1 small onion, chopped
- 1 tbsp finely chopped jalapeno pepper
- 6 saltine crackers, crushed
- 1 egg, beaten
- 1/2 C. shredded Cheddar cheese
- 1/4 tsp garlic powder
- Salt and pepper to taste
- 1/4 C. vegetable oil

Directions

1. Get a mixing bowl: Add the butter beans and press them with a spoon until they become mashed.
2. Add the onion, jalapeno pepper, crushed crackers, egg, cheese, garlic powder, salt, and pepper. Mix them well. Form the mix into 4 cakes.
3. Place a large skillet on medium heat. Add the oil and heat it. Cook in it the butter bean cakes for 6 min per side.
4. Assemble your burgers with your favorite toppings. Serve them right away.
5. Enjoy

THAI
Bell Bean Burgers

Prep Time: 15 mins
Total Time: 35 mins

Servings per Recipe: 4
Calories   198 kcal
Fat   3 g
Carbohydrates   33.1g
Protein   11.2 g
Cholesterol   46 mg
Sodium   607 mg

Ingredients

1 (16 ounce) can black beans, drained and rinsed
1/2 green bell pepper, cut into 2 inch pieces
1/2 onion, cut into wedges
3 cloves garlic, peeled
1 egg
1 tbsp chili powder
1 tbsp cumin
1 tsp Thai chili sauce or hot sauce
1/2 C. bread crumbs

Directions

1. Before you do anything heat the grill and grease it.
2. Get a mixing bowl: Add the black bean then press it with a potato masher or fork until it becomes well mashed.
3. Get a food processor: Add the bell pepper, onion, and garlic. Mix them well. Add the black beans and blend them smooth.
4. Get a small bowl: Add the egg, chili powder, cumin, and chili sauce. Whisk them well to make the sauce. Add the black bean mix with bread crumbs. Mix them well.
5. Shape the mix into 4 burger cakes. Cook them on the grill for 9 min on each side. Assemble your burgers with your favorite toppings. Serve them right away.
6. Enjoy.

Authentic Texas-Mexican Enchiladas

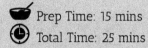

Prep Time: 15 mins
Total Time: 25 mins

Servings per Recipe: 5
Calories	933 kcal
Fat	59 g
Carbohydrates	69.1g
Protein	35.1 g
Cholesterol	108 mg
Sodium	1776 mg

Ingredients

- 2 (11.25 oz.) cans chili without beans
- 1 C. enchilada sauce
- 1/2 C. vegetable oil
- 1 tbsp chili powder
- 15 corn tortillas
- 1 lb. shredded Cheddar cheese
- 1 onion, chopped

Directions

1. Set your oven to 350 degrees F before doing anything else.
2. In a small pan, mix the chili and enchilada sauce on medium-low heat and heat, stirring occasionally.
3. In a small skillet, heat the vegetable oil and chili powder on medium heat and cook the tortillas, one at a time till they start to puff.
4. Transfer the tortillas on a plate and immediately sprinkle with 1/4 C. of the Cheddar cheese and 1 tbsp of the chopped onion in the center of each tortilla.
5. Roll the tortillas tightly around the mixture and place, seam-side down, into the bottom of a 13x9-inch baking dish.
6. Sprinkle about 2/3 of the remaining Cheddar cheese over the rolled enchiladas.
7. Place the warm chili mixture over the enchiladas evenly, followed by the remaining Cheddar cheese.
8. Cook in the oven for about 20-25 minutes.

TEX MEX
Breakfast Brunch

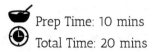 Prep Time: 10 mins
Total Time: 20 mins

Servings per Recipe: 6
Calories	283 kcal
Fat	12.2 g
Carbohydrates	30.8g
Protein	12.1 g
Cholesterol	196 mg
Sodium	661 mg

Ingredients

- 1 tbsp butter
- 1 (4 oz.) can chopped green chilis
- 1/2 tomato, chopped
- 6 large eggs
- 1/4 C. crushed tortilla chips
- 1/4 C. shredded sharp Cheddar cheese
- 6 (8 inch) flour tortillas
- 6 tbsp taco sauce

Directions

1. In a large skillet, melt the butter on medium heat and cook the green chilis and tomato for about 5 minutes.
2. Carefully, crack the eggs into the skillet and stir till the yolks break.
3. Cook, stirring for about 2-3 minutes.
4. Sprinkle the tortilla chips on top and mix with the eggs.
5. Move egg mixture to the side of the skillet and remove from the heat.
6. Immediately, sprinkle the Cheddar cheese over the egg mixture and keep aside, covered for about 5 minutes.
7. In a microwave-safe plate, place the flour tortillas and microwave for about 30 seconds.
8. Divide the egg mixture onto each tortilla and serve with a topping of the taco sauce.

Catalina's Salad

Prep Time: 5 mins
Total Time: 5 mins

Servings per Recipe: 10
Calories   542 kcal
Fat   33.1 g
Carbohydrates   52.7g
Protein   10.7 g
Cholesterol   12 mg
Sodium   1077 mg

Ingredients

1 (15 oz.) can pinto beans, drained and rinsed
1 (15 oz.) can black beans, rinsed and drained
1 1/2 C. shredded Cheddar and Monterey cheese blend
1 (10 oz.) package chopped romaine lettuce
3 tomatoes, chopped
1 (16 oz.) bottle Catalina salad dressing
1 (16 oz.) package corn chips

Directions

1. In a large bowl, mix together the pinto beans, black beans, cheese, lettuce and tomatoes.
2. Add 3/4 of the bottle of the dressing and mix well.
3. Add the corn chips before serving.

TUESDAY'S San Miguel Potatoes

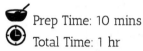

Prep Time: 10 mins
Total Time: 1 hr

Servings per Recipe: 4
Calories   420 kcal
Fat   13.2 g
Carbohydrates   60.3g
Protein   17.2 g
Cholesterol   25 mg
Sodium   681 mg

Ingredients

4 baking potatoes
1 tbsp vegetable oil
1 onion, chopped
1 large green bell pepper, chopped
1 (16 oz.) can chili beans in spicy sauce, undrained
1 tsp minced garlic
1 tbsp vegetarian Worcestershire sauce
1/2 tsp minced jalapeno peppers
1 C. shredded Monterey Jack cheese

Directions

1. With a sharp knife, scrub the potatoes and prick in several places.
2. Place the potatoes onto a paper towel and arrange in a microwave and microwave on high for about 8 minutes.
3. Turn and rotate the potatoes and microwave for about 8-10 minutes.
4. In a medium skillet, heat the oil on medium-high heat and sauté the onions and bell peppers till softened.
5. Stir in the beans, Worcestershire sauce, and jalapeño peppers.
6. Reduce the heat to low and simmer, covered for about 5-6 minutes.
7. Split the potatoes and top with the bean mixture.
8. Serve with a sprinkling of the cheese.

Chipotle Burgers

Prep Time: 15 mins
Total Time: 25 mins

Servings per Recipe: 3
Calories	691 kcal
Fat	44.2 g
Carbohydrates	35.4g
Protein	37.3 g
Cholesterol	129 mg
Sodium	1574 mg

Ingredients

- 1 lb. ground beef
- 3 tbsp chili seasoning mix
- 2 chipotle peppers in adobo sauce, minced
- 1/2 fluid oz. beer
- 1/4 C. mayonnaise
- 1 chipotle pepper in adobo sauce, minced
- 6 (1 oz.) slices white bread
- 6 (1/2 oz.) slices pepper jack cheese

Directions

1. In a bowl, mix together the ground beef, chili seasoning mix, 2 minced chipotle peppers with adobo sauce, and the beer.
2. Make 3 equal sized patties from the mixture.
3. In a small bowl, mix together the mayonnaise and 1 minced chipotle pepper with adobo sauce.
4. Spread the mayonnaise mixture over the bread slices evenly and top with a slice of pepper jack cheese.
5. Heat a large skillet over medium-high heat and cook the patties for about 5-7 minutes per side.
6. Place 1 burger over 1 slice of the bread and cover with the remaining slices to make sandwiches.
7. Drain the skillet, reserving 2 tbsp of the grease.
8. Heat the reserved grease in the skillet on medium-high heat and cook the sandwiches for about 1-2 minutes per side

MEXICAN
Mac n Cheese

Prep Time: 10 mins
Total Time: 30 mins

Servings per Recipe: 6
Calories   384 kcal
Fat   21.1 g
Carbohydrates   27.1g
Protein   19 g
Cholesterol   73 mg
Sodium   784 mg

Ingredients

1 lb. lean ground beef
1 (1.25 oz.) package taco seasoning mix
1 (7.3 oz.) package white Cheddar macaroni and cheese mix
2 tbsp butter
1/4 C. milk

Directions

1. Heat a large skillet on medium heat and cook the beef till browned completely.
2. Drain the excess grease from the skillet.
3. Add the taco seasoning and water according to seasoning package directions and simmer for about 10 minutes.
4. Remove from the heat and keep aside.
5. Prepare the macaroni and cheese according to package's directions, adding butter and milk as indicated.
6. Add the beef mixture and stir to combine.
7. Serve immediately.

Yogurt, Parmesan, Basil, Turkey Panini

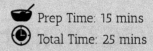

Prep Time: 15 mins
Total Time: 25 mins

Servings per Recipe: 4
Calories   279 kcal
Carbohydrates   26.9 g
Cholesterol   31 mg
Fat   9.7 g
Protein   22.1 g
Sodium   673 mg

Ingredients

3 tbsps reduced-fat mayonnaise
2 tbsps nonfat plain yogurt
2 tbsps shredded Parmesan cheese
2 tbsps chopped fresh basil
1 tsp lemon juice
Freshly ground pepper to taste
8 slices whole-wheat bread
8 oz thinly sliced reduced-sodium deli turkey
8 tomato slices
2 tsps canola oil

Directions

1. Heat up your Panini grill according to the instruction of the manufacturer.
2. Spread a mixture of mayonnaise, lemon juice, yogurt, Parmesan, basil and pepper over each half of the bread before putting turkey and tomato slices over the lower half, and closing it up to make a sandwich.
3. Put some butter on top and cook this Panini in the preheated grill for about 4 minutes or until the outside is golden brown.

CHICKEN BREAST, Zucchini, Pepper Panini

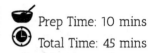

Prep Time: 10 mins
Total Time: 45 mins

Servings per Recipe: 2
Calories 597 kcal
Carbohydrates 32.5 g
Cholesterol 98 mg
Fat 34.1 g
Protein 36.3 g
Sodium 979 mg

Ingredients

1/2 C. Tuscan Dressing
2 (4 oz) boneless skinless chicken breast halves
1 red pepper, cut into strips
1 small zucchini, cut lengthwise in half, then sliced crosswise
4 slices Italian bread
1/2 C. KRAFT Shredded Low-Moisture Part-Skim Mozzarella Cheese
2 tbsps chopped fresh basil

Directions

1. Coat a mixture of vegetables and chicken with dressing before refrigerating it for at least thirty minutes.
2. Heat up your Panini grill according to the instruction of the manufacturer.
3. Cook chicken and vegetables over medium heat in a skillet for about 10 minutes or until tender.
4. Now fill up the bread slices with chicken, vegetables, basil and cheese.
5. Put some dressing on top of the bread and cook this Panini in the preheated grill for about five minutes or until the outside is golden brown.

Turkey Provolone Ciabatta

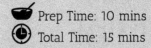

Prep Time: 10 mins
Total Time: 15 mins

Servings per Recipe: 1
Calories   792 kcal
Carbohydrates   66.7 g
Cholesterol   138 mg
Fat   34.9 g
Protein   53 g
Sodium   3267 mg

Ingredients

1 tbsp butter, or more if needed
2 slices ciabatta bread
6 slices deli-style sliced turkey breast
2 slices provolone cheese
3 sun-dried tomatoes packed in oil, drained and chopped

1/2 tsp Italian seasoning

Directions

1. Heat up your Panini grill according to the instruction of the manufacturer.
2. Spread butter over one lower side of bread and then put turkey, provolone cheese, Italian seasoning and sun dried tomatoes before closing it up to make a sandwich.
3. Put some margarine on top of each bread and cook this Panini in the preheated grill for about 5 minutes or until the outside is golden brown

DESSERT
Panini

Prep Time: 10 mins
Total Time: 25 mins

Servings per Recipe: 4
Calories   433 kcal
Carbohydrates   45.5 g
Cholesterol   3 mg
Fat   25.1 g
Protein   12.5 g
Sodium   507 mg

Ingredients

1 tsp butter
1/2 C. crunchy peanut butter
8 slices firm bread

1/2 C. semi-sweet chocolate chips

Directions

1. Heat up your Panini grill according to the instruction of the manufacturer.
2. Spread peanut butter and then chocolate over the lower half of the bread before closing it up with the upper half.
3. Put some butter on top and cook this Panini in the preheated grill for about 4 minutes or until the outside is golden brown.

Chipotle Pepper, Bacon, Spinach Panini

Prep Time: 20 mins
Total Time: 40 mins

Servings per Recipe: 6
Calories	699 kcal
Carbohydrates	65.1 g
Cholesterol	81 mg
Fat	33.2 g
Protein	34.5 g
Sodium	2276 mg

Ingredients

- 8 slices bacon
- 1 tbsp butter
- 2 cloves garlic, diced
- 1/2 red onion, thinly sliced
- 3 C. fresh spinach leaves
- 1/2 C. reduced-fat mayonnaise
- 2 chipotle peppers in adobo sauce, diced
- 1 tsp adobo sauce from chipotle peppers
- 8 (4 inch) pieces focaccia bread
- 4 slices provolone cheese
- 1/2 lb sliced deli turkey meat

Directions

1. Heat up your Panini grill according to the instruction of the manufacturer.
2. Cook bacon over medium heat until brown before draining it using a paper towel.
3. Now cook onion and garlic in hot butter for about ten minutes before adding spinach and cooking it for another three minutes.
4. Spread a mixture of mayonnaise, adobo sauce and diced chipotle peppers along with a slice of cheese over the upper half of the bread before putting turkey, a bacon and spinach mixture over the lower half and closing it up to make a sandwich.
5. Cook this Panini in the preheated grill for about 5 minutes or until the outside is golden brown.

DIJON, Roast Beef, Roquefort Panini

 Prep Time: 10 mins
Total Time: 25 mins

Servings per Recipe: 6
Calories 652 kcal
Carbohydrates 77.3 g
Cholesterol 96 mg
Fat 23.3 g
Protein 34.7 g
Sodium 2113 mg

Ingredients

3 tbsps unsalted butter
6 large shallots, sliced
salt and black pepper to taste
2 French baguettes, halved lengthwise
2 tbsps Dijon mustard, or to taste
1 C. Roquefort cheese, crumbled
1 lb thinly sliced deli roast beef
1/2 C. cold heavy cream
1 1/2 tbsps finely shredded horseradish root
1 pinch salt and white pepper to taste

Directions

1. Cook sliced shallots in hot butter for about ten minutes before adding salt and pepper.
2. Heat up your Panini grill according to the instruction of the manufacturer.
3. Spread Dijon mustard and Roquefort over the upper half of baguettes before putting roast beef and cooked shallots over the lower closing it up to make a sandwich.
4. Cook this Panini in the preheated grill for about 4 minutes or until the outside is golden brown.
5. Serve this with a mixt

Parmesan, Mozzarella, Chicken Cutlet Panini

Prep Time: 10 mins
Total Time: 25 mins

Servings per Recipe: 4
Calories 646 kcal
Carbohydrates 68.5 g
Cholesterol 125 mg
Fat 24.3 g
Protein 42.6 g
Sodium 1792 mg

Ingredients

1/4 C. flour
1 tsp garlic powder
1/2 tsp salt
1/4 tsp black pepper
1 egg, beaten
1 C. panko bread crumbs
1/4 C. Parmesan cheese
4 small chicken cutlets
2 tbsps olive oil
4 slices fresh mozzarella cheese
1/4 C. Parmesan cheese
8 thick slices artisanal-style bread
1 jar tomato sauce

Directions

1. Put a mixture of flour, salt, garlic powder and pepper, eggs and mixture of panko bread crumbs and parmesan cheese in three separate bowls.
2. Now coat chicken by dipping it in all the bowls and set it aside.
3. Now fry this chicken in hot olive oil for about four minutes each side.
4. Spread tomato sauce, slice of cheese and parmesan cheese over chicken placed on bread.
5. Now grill this in the Panini grill for 5 minutes or until the cheese has melted.
6. Serve.

SPINACH, Turkey Ciabatta Panini

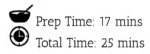

Prep Time: 17 mins
Total Time: 25 mins

Servings per Recipe: 6	
Calories	723 kcal
Carbohydrates	42.1 g
Cholesterol	62 mg
Fat	51.3 g
Protein	25.3 g
Sodium	1720 mg

Ingredients

1/2 ripe avocado
1/4 cup mayonnaise
2 ciabatta rolls
1 tablespoon olive oil, divided
2 slices provolone cheese
1 cup whole fresh spinach leaves, divided
1/4 pound honey turkey
2 roasted red peppers, sliced into strips

Directions

1. Heat up your Panini grill according to the instruction of the manufacturer.
2. Mash mayonnaise and avocado together very thoroughly in a bowl.
3. Now grill lower half of the bread brushed with olive oil for a few minutes before putting provolone cheese, turkey breast, spinach leaves, avocado mixture and roasted red pepper before closing it up to make a sandwich.
4. Spread cheese over the lower half of the bread before putting meat, mixture of vegetables and olives and remaining cheese before closing it up to make a sandwich.
5. Cook this Panini in the preheated grill for about seven minutes or until the outside is golden brown.

Balsamic, Parmesan, Mushroom Panini

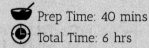 Prep Time: 40 mins
Total Time: 6 hrs

Servings per Recipe: 6
Calories	679 kcal
Carbohydrates	100.5 g
Cholesterol	46 mg
Fat	19 g
Protein	28.1 g
Sodium	1779 mg

Ingredients

- 2 red bell peppers
- 4 portobello mushroom caps
- 1 C. fat-free balsamic vinaigrette
- 4 (1/2 inch thick) slices eggplant, peeled
- 1 tsp garlic powder
- 1 tsp onion powder
- 2 tsps grated Parmesan cheese
- 8 slices focaccia bread
- 1/4 C. fat free ranch dressing
- 4 thin slices Swiss cheese
- 4 thin slices Asiago cheese

Directions

1. The distance of your broiler rack should be about 6 inches from the heat source before heating up.
2. Place peppers on a baking sheet after cutting them in half and removing seeds, stems and ribs.
3. Now cook this under the preheated broiler for about 10 minutes before letting it cool down for 20 minutes, while covered with a plastic wrap.
4. Refrigerate for the whole night
5. Coat Portobello mushroom caps with balsamic vinaigrette before refrigerating it too for the whole night.
6. Coat eggplant slices with onion powder and garlic powder before heating up the grill.
7. Now cook these eggplant slices and also Portobello mushrooms on the preheated grill for about four minutes each.
8. Spread ranch dressing over a slice of focaccia before placing a slice of cheese, eggplant, roasted pepper and Portobello mushroom over bread very evenly.
9. Close it up to form a sandwich.
10. Now cook these sandwiches on the grill for about 5 minutes or until you see that it is golden brown in color. Serve.

EMPANADAS
of Pineapple

Prep Time: 15 mins
Total Time: 1 hr 15 mins

Servings per Recipe: 12
Calories   292 kcal
Carbohydrates   38.3 g
Cholesterol   41 mg
Fat   14.7 g
Protein   2.5 g
Sodium   115 mg

Ingredients

3 cups white sugar
4 cups all-purpose flour
1 pound butter, softened and cut into pieces

2 (8 ounce) packages cream cheese, softened and cut into pieces
2 (10 ounce) jars pineapple preserves

Directions

1. Set your oven to 425 degrees F.
2. Mix flour and butter very thoroughly before adding cream cheese and kneading this dough until you see that it is no longer crumbly.
3. Make 1 inch balls from this dough and flat it out on a floured surface using rolling pin.
4. Fold it up around 1 tbsp preserve before pressing edges with fingers to seal.
5. Bake it in the preheated oven for about 20 minutes.

Mushroom Empanada

Prep Time: 15 mins
Total Time: 40 mins

Servings per Recipe: 20
Calories	115 kcal
Carbohydrates	11.6 g
Cholesterol	5 mg
Fat	6.3 g
Protein	3.7 g
Sodium	319 mg

Ingredients

- 2 (7.5 ounce) packages refrigerated buttermilk biscuits (not the layered varieties)
- Cornmeal for rolling
- 2 tbsps olive oil
- 1 medium onion, finely chopped
- 2 (10 ounce) packages white mushrooms, stems trimmed, cut into small dice
- 1 (4.5 ounce) can chopped green chilies
- 2 large garlic cloves, minced
- 2 tbsps minced fresh cilantro
- Salt and pepper to taste
- 4 ounces goat cheese, crumbled
- Olive oil, for brushing

Directions

1. Set your oven to 450 degrees F.
2. Cook onion in hot oil for about three minutes before adding mushrooms and cooking for another five minutes.
3. Now add chilies, pepper, garlic, salt and cilantro, and cook all this for another two minutes before turning the heat off and adding goat cheese.
4. Place biscuit on the cornmeal-coated surface and sprinkle cornmeal as required before rolling all these into five inch circles.
5. Fill each circle with the filling you just prepared before placing them on the baking sheet
6. Bake it for about 20 minutes or until you see that the top of each empanada has turned brown.

CHEESE
Empanada

🥣 Prep Time: 20 mins
🕐 Total Time: 40 mins

Servings per Recipe: 12
Calories	343 kcal
Carbohydrates	39 g
Cholesterol	57 mg
Fat	13.8 g
Protein	14.8 g
Sodium	287 mg

Ingredients

3 cups all-purpose flour
1 tsp baking powder
1/2 tsp salt
2 tbsps lard
1 cup whole milk
1 egg, well beaten

1 cup queso chanco (or Swiss cheese or Havarti), cut into 1/2-inch cubes

Directions

1. Set your oven to 375 degrees F.
2. Combine flour, salt, hot milk and baking powder very thoroughly before kneading it until you see that the dough is smooth and elastic.
3. Cut the dough into four inch circles before filling it up with mound of cheese.
4. Press the edges of the empanadas with folk before placing them in the baking sheet.
5. Brush all these empanadas with the beaten egg before baking it for about 20 minutes or until you see that the top of each empanada has turned brown.
6. Serve.

Picadillo Empanada

Prep Time: 15 mins
Total Time: 40 mins

Servings per Recipe: 20
Calories   140 kcal
Carbohydrates   14.3 g
Cholesterol   13 mg
Fat   6.6 g
Protein   6.4 g
Sodium   313 mg

Ingredients

- 2 (7.5 ounce) packages refrigerated buttermilk biscuits (not the layered varieties)
- Cornmeal for rolling
- 2 tbsps olive oil
- 1 medium onion, finely chopped
- 1/2 medium Granny Smith apple, cut into small dice
- 1/4 tsp ground cinnamon
- 1/8 tsp ground cloves
- 2 cups shredded meat from a rotisserie chicken
- 1 (16 ounce) can crushed tomatoes
- 1/4 cup seedless raisins
- 1/4 cup chopped pimento-stuffed olives
- 2 large garlic cloves, minced
- 1/4 cup toasted slivered almonds
- Salt and pepper, to taste
- Olive oil, for brushing

Directions

1. Set oven to 450 degrees F.
2. Cook onion and apple in hot oil for about four minutes before adding spices and cooking for another 30 seconds.
3. Now add olives, chicken, raisins and tomatoes, and cook for another seven minutes before adding garlic, pepper, almonds and salt.
4. Place biscuit on the cornmeal-coated surface and sprinkle cornmeal as required before rolling all these into five inch circles.
5. Fill each circle with the filling you just prepared before placing them on the baking sheet
6. Bake it for about 20 minutes or until you see that the top of each empanada has turned brown.

EMPANADAS
In Argentina

Prep Time: 15 mins
Total Time: 40 mins

Servings per Recipe: 10
Calories	498 kcal
Carbohydrates	27.7 g
Cholesterol	73 mg
Fat	36.8 g
Protein	14.7 g
Sodium	326 mg

Ingredients

- 1/2 cup shortening
- 2 onions, chopped
- 1 pound lean ground beef
- 2 tsps Hungarian sweet paprika
- 3/4 tsp hot paprika
- 1/2 tsp crushed red pepper flakes
- 1 tsp ground cumin
- 1 tbsp distilled white vinegar
- 1/4 cup raisins
- 1/2 cup pitted green olives, chopped
- 2 hard-cooked eggs, chopped
- salt to taste
- 1 (17.5 ounce) package frozen puff pastry sheets, thawed

Directions

1. Cook onion and shortening in hot oil for a few minutes before adding sweet paprika, crushed red pepper flakes, hot paprika and salt.
2. Cook meat in boiling water for some time before transferring this to a dish and adding salt, vinegar and cumin.
3. Mix this meat mixture with the onion mixture in a bowl and let it cool down.
4. Cut ten circles from the pastry dough before placing that meat mixture, hard-boiled egg, raisins and olives on each one of them.
5. Now fold it around this filling very neatly to form a shape that resembles half-moon.
6. Press the edges with a folk.
7. Set your oven to 375 degrees F and place these empanadas in the baking sheet.
8. Brush all these empanadas with the beaten egg before baking it for about 30 minutes or until you see that the top of each empanada has turned brown.
9. Serve.

Classical Empanadas II

Prep Time: 30 mins
Total Time: 1 hr

Servings per Recipe: 22
Calories	105 kcal
Carbohydrates	11.7 g
Cholesterol	32 mg
Fat	5.6 g
Protein	2.3 g
Sodium	102 mg

Ingredients

- 1 recipe pastry for a 9 inch double crust pie
- 2 large potatoes, peeled and cubed
- 2 tbsps olive oil
- 2 onions, diced
- 3 hard-cooked eggs, chopped
- 1/4 cup chopped green olives
- 1/2 cup raisins
- salt and pepper to taste
- 2 eggs, beaten

Directions

1. Set your oven to 375 degrees F.
2. Cook potatoes in boiling water for about five minutes to get it tendered.
3. Cook onion in hot oil for about 5 minutes before adding cooked potatoes and cooking it for another ten minutes or until you see that the potatoes are lightly brown.
4. Transfer this to bowl and stir in raisins, salt, pepper, hard-cooked eggs and olives.
5. Cut ten circles from the pastry dough after rolling it up on a floured surface.
6. Now fold it around this filling very neatly to form a shape that resembles half-moon.
7. Press the edges with a folk and place them in the baking sheet.
8. Brush all these empanadas with the beaten egg before baking it for about 30 minutes or until you see that the top of each empanada has turned brown.

CLASSICAL
Empanadas III

Prep Time: 45 mins
Total Time: 1 hr 20 mins

Servings per Recipe: 20
Calories   140 kcal
Carbohydrates   14.3 g
Cholesterol   13 mg
Fat   6.6 g
Protein   6.4 g
Sodium   313 mg

Ingredients

1 tbsp Goya Extra Virgin Olive Oil
1/2 pound ground beef
1/2 medium yellow onion, finely chopped
1/4 cup Goya Tomato Sauce
6 Goya Spanish Olives Stuffed with Minced Pimientos, thinly sliced
1 packet Sazon Goya with Coriander and Annatto
2 tbsps Goya Sofrito
1 tsp Goya Minced Garlic
1/2 tsp Goya Dried Oregano
Goya Ground Black Pepper, to taste
1 (14 ounce) package Goya Discos (yellow or white), thawed
Goya Corn Oil, for frying

Directions

1. Cook beef in hot oil for about ten minutes before adding onions and cooking it for another five minutes.
2. Now add black pepper, oregano, sofrito, garlic, tomato sauce, sazon and olives before turning down the heat to medium and cooking it for another 15 minutes.
3. On a lightly floured surface, roll out discos until you see that it is half inch in diameter before folding it around the meat mixture to form a half-moon like shape.
4. Press folk to the edges of these empanadas before deep frying them in hot oil in batches for about 6 minutes each, while turning only once.
5. Serve.

Squash Empanada

Prep Time: 15 mins
Total Time: 40 mins

Servings per Recipe: 16
Calories   308 kcal
Carbohydrates   27.7 g
Cholesterol   27 mg
Fat   20.1 g
Protein   5.4 g
Sodium   286 mg

Ingredients

1 tbsp extra-virgin olive oil
1 tbsp butter
3 cloves garlic, minced
1 (1 inch) piece fresh ginger, minced
2 kohlrabi bulbs, peeled and cubed
salt and pepper to taste
1 large yellow squash, cubed
2 green onions, chopped
1/2 cup chopped fresh spinach
1 pinch ground nutmeg
1 egg
1 tsp water
1 (15 ounce) package pastry for a 9 inch double crust pie

Directions

1. Set oven to 425 degrees F.
2. Cook ginger and garlic in hot oil for about three minutes before adding kohlrabi, pepper and salt and cooking it for another four minutes.
3. Now add yellow squash and cook it for another four minutes before adding green onion, nutmeg pepper, salt and spinach, and cooking it one more minute.
4. Roll out the pie crust on a floured surface and cut sixteen 6-inch circles by using cookie cutter before folding it up around the kohlrabi mixture.
5. Press folk to the edges of the empanadas to seal them and then place them in the baking dish
6. Bake it for about seven minutes or until you see that the top of each empanada has turned brown

EMPANADAS
From Chile

Prep Time: 20 mins
Total Time: 1 hr 10 mins

Servings per Recipe: 12
Calories	530 kcal
Carbohydrates	54.2 g
Cholesterol	113 mg
Fat	27.9 g
Protein	16.1 g
Sodium	653 mg

Ingredients

- 1 tbsp butter
- 1 large onion, chopped
- 1 tsp minced garlic
- 1 tsp dried oregano
- 1 tsp cumin
- 1/2 tsp salt
- 1/2 tsp ground black pepper
- 1 pound ground pork
- 3 hard-cooked eggs, chopped
- 1 cup raisins
- 1 cup chopped black olives
- 1 cup water
- 1 tsp cornstarch
- 1 cup lukewarm milk
- 1 cup shortening, melted
- 5 cups all-purpose flour
- 2 tsps salt
- 2 eggs, beaten

Directions

1. Set oven to 425 degrees F.
2. Cook onion, oregano, pepper, garlic, salt and cumin in hot butter for about seven minutes before adding ground pork and cooking it for ten more minutes or until you see that it is completely brown.
3. Now add olives, mixture of cornstarch and water, eggs and raisins into it and cook it until you see that the liquid is thick enough.
4. Combine the mixture of milk and melted butter, and mixture of salt and flour together in a large sized bowl until you see that it is well mixed and has taken a form of dough.
5. Cut circles using cookie cutter after rolling dough on a floured surface, and fold these circles around the pork mixture.
6. Press folk to the edges of the empanadas to seal them and then place them in the baking dish
7. Brush these empanadas with beaten egg and bake it for about seven minutes or until you see that the top of each empanada has turned brown.

Classical Empanada IV

🥣 Prep Time: 30 mins
🕐 Total Time: 1 hr 30 mins

Servings per Recipe: 10
Calories   415 kcal
Carbohydrates   49.7 g
Cholesterol   24 mg
Fat   19.7 g
Protein   11.3 g
Sodium   312 mg

Ingredients

- 1/2 tsp salt
- 2/3 cup shortening
- 6 tbsps water
- 2 1/2 cups peeled, cored and sliced apples
- 1 cup white sugar
- 1 tsp ground cinnamon
- 1/2 tsp ground nutmeg
- 1 yellow onion
- 1 green bell pepper
- 1 tbsp olive oil
- 8 ounces tomato paste
- 1/2 cup water
- 1 tbsp distilled white vinegar
- 1 pound lean steak, cut into 1 inch cubes

Directions

1. Combine flour, salt, water and shortening very thoroughly to form dough.
2. Roll this out on a floured surface before cutting it into four inch circles.
3. Cook the mixture of fruit, nutmeg, sugar and cinnamon until very hot.
4. Coat meat with the mixture of onion, tomato sauce, green pepper, water and vinegar cooked in hot oil for about 20 minutes.
5. Place any of the above mixture in the center of dough circle before pressing its edge with a fork and baking it for ten minutes.
6. Serve

BANANA
Empanada

Prep Time: 20 mins
Total Time: 55 mins

Servings per Recipe: 4
Calories   157 mg
Carbohydrates   49.8 g
Cholesterol
Fat   19.9 g
Protein   5.6 g
Sodium   157 mg

Ingredients

1/4 cup raisins
2 1/2 cups all-purpose flour
1/2 tsp salt
3/4 cup shortening
2 tbsps plain yogurt
1/2 cup cold water

4 large ripe bananas, coarsely chopped
1/2 tsp ground cinnamon, or to taste
1 tbsp cold water
1 egg white

Directions

1. Set oven to 425 degrees F.
2. Let the raisins stand in hot water for about 30 minutes.
3. Combine flour, salt, water, yoghurt and shortening very thoroughly to form dough.
4. Roll out dough on floured surface before cutting four 8x8 inch squares.
5. Place mixture of chopped bananas, raisins and cinnamon to the center of each square, while leaving some space to roll it up.
6. Press edges with the help of folk to seal it properly
7. Brush these empanadas with beaten egg and bake it for about thirty minutes or until you see that the top of each empanada has turned brown.
8. Enjoy.

Bacon and Onions Quesadillas

Prep Time: 15 mins
Total Time: 35 mins

Servings per Recipe: 4
Calories   449 kcal
Fat   21.1 g
Carbohydrates   47.7 g
Protein   15.5 g
Cholesterol   37 mg
Sodium   1286 mg

Ingredients

- 2 tbsps olive oil
- 1/2 large yellow onion, sliced thin
- 6 slices bacon, minced
- 1 tbsp brown sugar
- 8 (10 inch) flour tortillas
- 1 C. spicy barbeque sauce
- 1/4 C. diced fresh cilantro
- 2 C. shredded Cheddar cheese

Directions

1. Stir fry your onions for 7 mins until tender in 1 tablespoon of olive oil. Then combine in brown sugar, and bacon. Continue frying until the bacon is crispy. Take everything out of the pan.
2. Layer the following on a tortilla: one fourth bbq sauce, 1 tbsp cilantro, 1/4 bacon, half of your cheddar, and 1 tortilla.
3. Cook the quesadilla in a pan for 2 mins per side in 1 tsp of olive oil.
4. Repeat for all ingredients. Then before serving cut the quesadillas in half.
5. Enjoy.

RESTAURANT STYLE
Quesadilla Dipping Sauce

 Prep Time: 10 mins
Total Time: 4 hrs 10 mins

Servings per Recipe: 18
Calories   93 kcal
Fat   9.8 g
Carbohydrates   1.5g
Protein   0.2 g
Cholesterol   5 mg
Sodium   126 mg

Ingredients

1 C. mayonnaise (such as Hellman's(R))
3 tbsps canned minced jalapeno peppers, drained (reserve juice)
1 tbsp white sugar
2 tsps paprika
2 tsps ground cumin
1/2 tsp cayenne pepper
1/2 tsp garlic powder
1/4 tsp salt

Directions

1. Get a bowl, mix: salt, mayo, garlic powder, jalapenos, cayenne, 3 tbsps of pepper juice, cumin, paprika, and sugar.
2. Place a lid on the bowl or some plastic wrap and chill in the fridge for 8 hours.
3. Enjoy.

Mediterranean Style Quesadillas

Prep Time: 15 mins
Total Time: 40 mins

Servings per Recipe: 4
Calories   346 kcal
Fat   18.5 g
Carbohydrates   33.4g
Protein   11.7 g
Cholesterol   23 mg
Sodium   493 mg

Ingredients

- 1 onion, diced
- 6 large cremini mushrooms, diced
- 2 large cloves garlic, minced
- salt and ground black pepper to taste
- 2 tbsps extra-virgin olive oil
- 2 tsps balsamic vinegar
- 1/4 C. herbed goat cheese (chevre)
- 4 tsps whipped cream cheese
- 4 flour tortillas
- 1/3 C. shredded mozzarella cheese

Directions

1. Stir fry in olive oil for 7 mins: mushrooms, black pepper, onions, salt, and garlic, and balsamic vinegar.
2. Get a bowl, mix: goat and cream cheese.
3. Get another pan and toast a tortilla for 2 mins per side.
4. Then layer the following on one side of it: one fourth cheese mix, one fourth mushrooms, one fourth mozzarella.
5. Fold to form a quesadilla. Heat this for 5 mins in the pan. Then repeat for all ingredients.
6. Enjoy.

HONEY BBQ Chicken Quesadillas

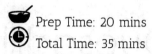

Prep Time: 20 mins
Total Time: 35 mins

Servings per Recipe: 8
Calories 411 kcal
Fat 14.3 g
Carbohydrates 46.2g
Protein 23.2 g
Cholesterol 48 mg
Sodium 753 mg

Ingredients

2 tbsps vegetable oil, divided
1 onion, sliced into rings
1 tbsp honey
2 skinless, boneless chicken breast halves - cut into strips
1/2 C. barbeque sauce
1/2 C. shredded sharp Cheddar cheese
1/2 C. shredded Monterey Jack cheese
8 (10 inch) flour tortillas

Directions

1. Set your oven to 350 degrees before doing anything else.
2. Stir fry your onions for 5 mins in 1 tbsp of olive oil. Then add your honey and cook for 1 more min, put the onions in a bowl.
3. Now add your chicken to the pan and also some more oil and cook until fully done. Add in some bbq sauce and stir everything.
4. Layer the following on four tortillas: onions, Monterey, chicken, cheese, and another tortilla.
5. Cook the contents in the oven for 22 mins. Before serving cut them in half.
6. Enjoy.

Cinnamon and Apples Quesadillas

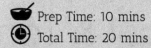

Prep Time: 10 mins
Total Time: 20 mins

Servings per Recipe: 4
Calories   369 kcal
Fat   17.9 g
Carbohydrates   38.4g
Protein   13.8 g
Cholesterol   47 mg
Sodium   652 mg

Ingredients

1 1/2 tsps butter, divided
2 (12 inch) flour tortillas
6 oz. Brie cheese, rind removed and cheese thinly sliced
1 sweet-tart apple, such as Fugi or Gala, thinly sliced
1 tbsp brown sugar
1/4 tsp ground cinnamon

Directions

1. Toast 1 tortilla in 3/4 of a tsp of butter.
2. Layer some brie and apple on the tortilla then some cinnamon and sugar, top with another tortilla.
3. Heat everything for 4 mins.
4. Put another 3/4 of a tsp of butter on the tortilla and then turn it over and cook for 4 more mins.
5. Before serving cut the tortillas in half.
6. Enjoy.

CHIPOTLE Basil & Tomato Quesadillas

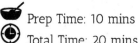
Prep Time: 10 mins
Total Time: 20 mins

Servings per Recipe: 8
Calories 366 kcal
Fat 20.2 g
Carbohydrates 31.1g
Protein 14.2 g
Cholesterol 38 mg
Sodium 733 mg

Ingredients

8 (8 inch) flour tortillas
2 C. shredded Mexican blend cheese
1 (10 oz.) can minced Tomatoes with Chipotle
8 slices bacon, cooked and crumbled
1/2 C. diced fresh basil
2 tbsps vegetable oil
Sour cream

Directions

1. One side of each tortilla layer: 1 tbsp of bacon, one fourth C. cheese, 1 tablespoon of basil, 2 tbsps of minced tomatoes.
2. Fold the other side of the tortilla to form a quesadilla. Toast each quesadilla for 2 mins per side in a pan coated with nonstick spray.
3. Repeat this process for all ingredients.
4. Before serving cut the quesadillas in half.
5. Enjoy.

Steak and Onions Quesadillas

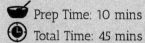

Prep Time: 10 mins
Total Time: 45 mins

Servings per Recipe: 4
Calories	927 kcal
Fat	36.4 g
Carbohydrates	101.3g
Protein	46.3 g
Cholesterol	108 mg
Sodium	1985 mg

Ingredients

- 1 (1 lb) beef top sirloin, thinly sliced
- 2 small onions, sliced
- 2 green bell peppers, sliced
- 1 C. barbeque sauce (such as Bull's-Eye(R) Texas-Style Bold Barbeque Sauce)
- 8 (10 inch) flour tortillas
- 2 C. shredded Cheddar cheese

Directions

1. Set your oven to 425 degrees before doing anything else.
2. Stir fry your beef for 9 mins then add in your bell peppers and onions. Cook for 11 more mins. Then add bbq sauce and stir it for a bit.
3. Let the contents lightly simmer for 12 mins.
4. Get a casserole dish or baking sheet and layer the following on 4 tortillas: beef, cheddar, and another tortilla.
5. Cook everything in the oven for 12 mins.
6. Then turn over each quesadilla and cook for 6 more mins.
7. Enjoy.

AUTHENTIC Mexican Quesadillas

Prep Time: 30 mins
Total Time: 50 mins

Servings per Recipe: 4
Calories	706 kcal
Fat	35.4 g
Carbohydrates	52g
Protein	46.6 g
Cholesterol	115 mg
Sodium	1301 mg

Ingredients

8 (8 inch) flour tortillas
3 green chili peppers
Pico de Gallo:
1 green bell pepper, halved, divided
2 small tomatoes, minced
1 small onion, divided
3 fresh jalapeno peppers, minced
2 tbsps diced fresh cilantro
2 tbsps tomato juice
1 lime, juiced
1 clove garlic, minced
1/2 tsp salt
1/2 tsp ground black pepper
1/4 tsp garlic salt
Filling:
3 tbsps extra-light olive oil, divided

2 cooked skinless, boneless chicken breast halves, minced
7 mushrooms, sliced
1 tbsp chili powder
1/2 tsp dried oregano
1 pinch garlic salt
1 pinch ground black pepper
1/3 C. red enchilada sauce, or more to taste
Quesadilla:
1/2 C. shredded pepper jack cheese
1/2 C. shredded Cheddar cheese
4 (10 inch) flour tortillas

Directions

1. For 5 mins roast chili peppers under a preheated broiler to get the skins toasted. Once toasted place them in a resealable bag.
2. After setting them aside for 10 mins remove the outside skins from the peppers. Now mince them.
3. Dice half of your onions and bell peppers and then combine them with the following in a bowl: one fourth tsp of garlic salt, one half tsp pepper, tomatoes, salt, jalapenos, garlic, cilantro, lime juice, and tomato juice.
4. Place a lid on the bowl and place the contents in the fridge.
5. Dice the remaining peppers and onions and stir fry them for 7 mins along with

mushrooms and chicken in 1 tbsp of olive oil.
6. Combine with the mushrooms and chicken: some black pepper, green chilies, some salt, oregano, and chili powder.
7. Cook for 1 min. Then add in some enchilada sauce.
8. Layer the following on one side of each tortilla: vegetable mix, pepper jack cheese.
9. Then fold it in half to form a quesadilla.
10. Coat the quesadilla with 2 tbsps of olive oil and toast them in a pan for 2 mins per side.
11. Before serving cut the quesadillas in half.
12. Enjoy.

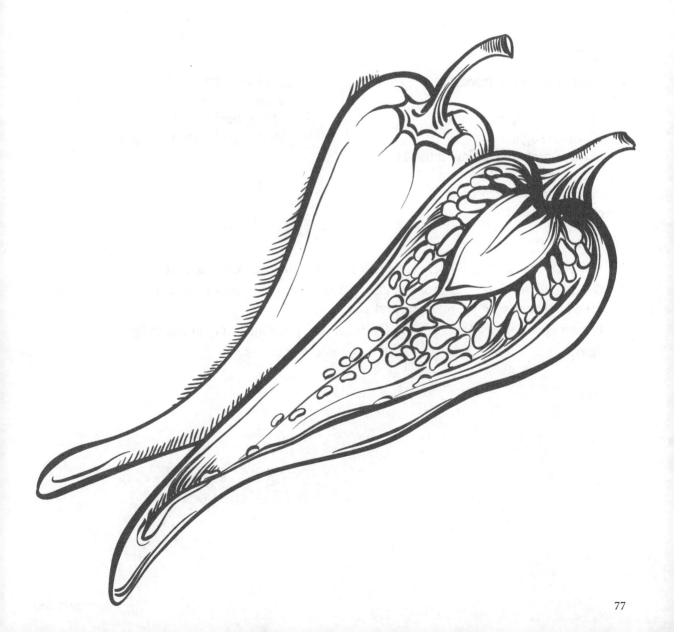

MACARONI
Salad

🥣 Prep Time: 20 mins
🕐 Total Time: 4 hrs 30 mins

Servings per Recipe: 10
Calories	390 kcal
Fat	18.7 g
Carbohydrates	49.3g
Protein	6.8 g
Cholesterol	8 mg
Sodium	529 mg

Ingredients

- 4 C. uncooked elbow macaroni
- 1 C. mayonnaise
- 1/4 C. distilled white vinegar
- 2/3 C. white sugar
- 2 1/2 tbsps prepared yellow mustard
- 1 1/2 tsps salt
- 1/2 tsp ground black pepper
- 1 large onion, diced
- 2 stalks celery, diced
- 1 green bell pepper, seeded and diced
- 1/4 C. grated carrot
- 2 tbsps diced pimento peppers

Directions

1. Boil your macaroni in water and salt for 9 mins then remove the liquids.
2. Get a bowl, combine: macaroni, onions, pimentos, celery, carrots, black pepper, mayo, salt, green peppers, vinegar, mustard, and sugar.
3. Place a covering of plastic around the bowl and put everything in the fridge for 5 hrs.
4. Enjoy.

Classical Potato Salad

Prep Time: 1 hr
Total Time: 2 hrs

Servings per Recipe: 12
Calories   430 kcal
Fat   36.9 g
Carbohydrates   16.2 g
Protein   9.5 g
Cholesterol   121 mg
Sodium   536 mg

Ingredients

2 lbs clean, scrubbed new red potatoes
6 eggs
1 lb turkey bacon
1 onion, finely diced
1 stalk celery, finely diced
2 C. mayonnaise
salt and pepper to taste

Directions

1. Boil your potatoes in water and salt for 20 mins then remove the liquids.
2. Once the potatoes are no longer hot, chop them, with the skins.
3. Now get your eggs boiling in water for 60 secs, place a lid on the pot, and shut the heat.
4. Let the eggs sit for 15 mins. Then remove the shells and dice them.
5. Stir fry your bacon until it is crispy then break it into pieces.
6. Get a bowl, combine: black pepper, celery, salt, eggs, mayo, onion, and bacon.
7. Place a covering of plastic around the bowl and put everything in the fridge for 65 mins.
8. Enjoy.

EASY
Spinach Salad

Prep Time: 10 mins
Total Time: 10 mins

Servings per Recipe: 8
Calories	235 kcal
Fat	15.9 g
Carbohydrates	22.8g
Protein	3.6 g
Cholesterol	0 mg
Sodium	69 mg

Ingredients

2 bunches spinach, rinsed and torn into bite-size pieces
4 C. sliced strawberries
1/2 C. vegetable oil
1/4 C. white wine vinegar
1/2 C. white sugar
1/4 tsp paprika
2 tbsps sesame seeds
1 tbsp poppy seeds

Directions

1. Get a bowl, combine: strawberries and spinach.
2. Get a 2nd bowl, combine: poppy seeds, oil, sesame seeds, vinegar, paprika, and sugar.
3. Combine both bowls then serve the salad.
4. Enjoy.

Pecan Chicken Salad

Prep Time: 15 mins
Total Time: 15 mins

Servings per Recipe: 12
Calories	315 kcal
Fat	23.1 g
Carbohydrates	15.2g
Protein	13.9 g
Cholesterol	42 mg
Sodium	213 mg

Ingredients

- 4 C. cubed, cooked chicken meat
- 1 C. mayonnaise
- 1 tsp paprika
- 1 1/2 C. dried cranberries
- 1 C. diced celery
- 2 green onions, diced
- 1/2 C. minced green bell pepper
- 1 C. diced pecans
- 1 tsp seasoning salt
- ground black pepper to taste

Directions

1. Get a bowl, combine: seasoned salt, paprika, and mayo. Get this mix smooth then add in: the nuts, celery, onion, bell peppers, and cranberries.
2. Mix everything again then add the chicken and black pepper.
3. Place the contents in the fridge for 65 mins then serve.
4. Enjoy.

PEAR and Cheese Salad

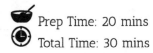

Prep Time: 20 mins
Total Time: 30 mins

Servings per Recipe: 6
Calories   426 kcal
Fat   31.6 g
Carbohydrates   33.1g
Protein   8 g
Cholesterol   21 mg
Sodium   654 mg

Ingredients

1 head leaf lettuce, torn into bite-size pieces
3 pears - peeled, cored and diced
5 oz. Roquefort cheese, crumbled
1 avocado - peeled, pitted, and diced
1/2 C. thinly sliced green onions
1/4 C. white sugar
1/2 C. pecans
1/3 C. olive oil

3 tbsps red wine vinegar
1 1/2 tsps white sugar
1 1/2 tsps prepared mustard
1 clove garlic, diced
1/2 tsp salt
fresh ground black pepper to taste

Directions

1. Toast your pecans and 1/4 C. of sugar, while stirring, until the sugar melts and coats the pecans.
2. Then place the pecans on some parchment paper.
3. Blend the following in a blender until smooth: pepper, oil, salt, 1.5 tsp sugar, diced garlic, and mustard.
4. Get a bowl, combine: green onions, lettuce, avocados, pears, blue cheese, and dressing mix.
5. Stir the contents then add in your pecans.
6. Enjoy.

Tuna Salad

Prep Time: 10 mins
Total Time: 10 mins

Servings per Recipe: 4
Calories	228 kcal
Fat	17.3 g
Carbohydrates	5.3g
Protein	13.4 g
Cholesterol	24 mg
Sodium	255 mg

Ingredients

1 (7 oz.) can white tuna, drained and flaked
6 tbsps mayonnaise or salad dressing
1 tbsp Parmesan cheese
3 tbsps sweet pickle relish
1/8 tsp dried minced onion flakes
1/4 tsp curry powder
1 tbsp dried parsley
1 tsp dried dill weed
1 pinch garlic powder

Directions

1. Get a bowl, combine: onion flakes, tuna, parmesan, and mayo.
2. Stir the contents until they are smooth then add the garlic powder, curry powder, dill, and parsley.
3. Stir the contents again to evenly distribute the spices.
4. Enjoy over toasted buns or crackers.

LATIN
Corn Salad

🥣 Prep Time: 25 mins
🕐 Total Time: 25 mins

Servings per Recipe: 6
Calories   391 kcal
Fat   24.5 g
Carbohydrates   35.1g
Protein   10.5 g
Cholesterol   0 mg
Sodium   830 mg

Ingredients

1/3 C. fresh lime juice
1/2 C. olive oil
1 clove garlic, minced
1 tsp salt
1/8 tsp ground cayenne pepper
2 (15 oz.) cans black beans, rinsed and drained
1 1/2 C. frozen corn kernels
1 avocado - peeled, pitted and diced

1 red bell pepper, diced
2 tomatoes, diced
6 green onions, thinly sliced
1/2 C. diced fresh cilantro

Directions

1. Get a mason jar and add in: cayenne, lime juice, salt, garlic, and olive oil.
2. Place a lid on the jar tightly and shake everything.
3. Now get a large bowl, combine: cilantro, beans, green onions, corn, tomatoes, bell pepper, and avocado.
4. Combine in the lime mix then toss the contents.
5. Enjoy.

Egg Salad

Prep Time: 10 mins
Total Time: 35 mins

Servings per Recipe: 4
Calories	344 kcal
Fat	31.9 g
Carbohydrates	2.3g
Protein	< 13 g
Cholesterol	382 mg
Sodium	1351 mg

Ingredients

- 8 eggs
- 1/2 C. mayonnaise
- 1 tsp prepared yellow mustard
- 1/4 C. diced green onion
- salt and pepper to taste
- 1/4 tsp paprika

Directions

1. Boil your eggs in water for 2 mins then place a lid on the pot and let the contents sit for 15 mins. Once the eggs have cooled remove their shells and dice them.
2. Now get a bowl, combine: green onions, eggs, mustard, and mayo.
3. Stir the mix until it is smooth then add in the paprika, pepper, and salt.
4. Stir the contents again then enjoy with toasted buns.

ENJOY THE RECIPES?
KEEP ON COOKING WITH 6 MORE FREE COOKBOOKS!

Visit our website and simply enter your email address to join the club and receive your 6 cookbooks.

http://booksumo.com/magnet

https://www.instagram.com/booksumopress/

https://www.facebook.com/booksumo/

CPSIA information can be obtained
at www.ICGtesting.com
Printed in the USA
LVHW050328030223
738591LV00008B/182